$11.50   94-32

B
GRE   Leder, Jane Mersky
             Wayne Gretsky.

DATE DUE

OC 27 94			

Wayne Gretzky

By
Jane Mersky Leder

Edited By
Dr. Howard Schroeder
Professor in Reading and Language Arts
Dept. of Elementary Education
Mankato State University

Produced & Designed By

Baker Street Productions, Ltd.

CRESTWOOD HOUSE
Mankato, Minnesota
U.S.A.

LIBRARY OF CONGRESS CATALOGING IN PUBLICATION DATA

Leder, Jane Mersky.
 Wayne Gretzky.

 SUMMARY: A sports biography of Wayne Gretzky, who, though "small", has become a spectacular hockey player.
 1. Gretzky, Wayne, 1961-   —Juvenile literature. 2. Hockey players—Canada—Biography—Juvenile literature. 3. National Hockey League—Juvenile literature. [1. Gretzky, Wayne, 1961-   . 2. Hockey players] I. Schroeder, Howard. II. Baker Street Productions. III. Title.
 GV848.5.G73L43   1985   796.96'2'0924   [B]   [92]   84-14980
 ISBN 0-89686-255-0

International Standard Book Number: 0-89686-255-0	Library of Congress Catalog Card Number: 84-14980

PHOTO CREDITS

Cover: Focus on Sports (Richard Pilling)
Wide World Photos: 4, 13, 17, 18-19, 42-43, 47
United Press: 7, 24-25, 26, 38-39
Focus on Sports: 11, 15, 21
Sports Illustrated: (Paul Bereswill) 28, 40, 41, 45; (John Iacono) 31, 33, 34, 36

Hwy. 66 South, Box 3427
Mankato, MN 56002-3427

TABLE
OF
CONTENTS

Wayne plays a thinking game.

ONE STEP AHEAD

Wayne Gretzky does not look like a professional hockey player. He weighs only 170 pounds, much less than most hockey pros. He is not very muscular, either. Other players lift weights, run, and ride exercise bikes. Wayne doesn't even like to do pushups! When he and his teammates were tested for upper body strength, Wayne placed last. But Wayne's style depends on his mind, not on his body.

Wayne plays a thinking game of hockey. He stays away from the violence of the sport. Some players enjoy the fights on the ice. Wayne tries not to get involved. He's more interested in the skill of the game. He can swat pucks out of the air, as if they were beach balls. His passing is great. And he thinks on another level. He is always one step ahead of the game. Wayne thinks more like a chess master than a hockey player.

Wayne seems to be able to see everything at once when he is on the ice. It's as if he can see in slow motion. The other players are usually a beat behind him. He can hold the puck just a bit longer or release it just a bit sooner. He is able to thread the puck through a group of players. "I've been doing this since I was six years old," said Wayne. "Now I don't even have to think when I'm on the ice. My plan just comes to me."

Doing what just comes to him has made Wayne Gretzky the most popular hockey player since Bobby Orr. He has captured the imagination of hockey fans all over the world. In his first four seasons in the National Hockey League (NHL), Wayne set thirty-seven records! He scored points in thirty straight games and broke all single-season scoring records. More than all the records, though, Wayne set his sights on just one thing—winning the Stanley Cup.

BORN TO PLAY HOCKEY

In most Canadian cities, toddlers learn to skate before they can spell their names. Wayne was no different. He just learned faster and better than most children.

Wayne was born in Brantford, Ontario on January 26, 1961. He was the first of four children. His father, Walter, worked for the telephone company. When Walter was younger, he had played junior hockey. He was not a great player. But Walter never forgot his dreams of being a star. When Wayne was just two years old, Walter decided to make Wayne the hockey star in the family.

First, Walter taught his son how to skate. Before long, he bought the smallest hockey stick he could find. Then he cut it down even further. Then he began teaching Wayne how to use the stick.

Walter was very serious about his son learning how to play hockey. He even built a skating rink for Wayne in the backyard! Lights were put up so they could play at night. Wayne and his father spent many long hours on the rink. Walter worked his son hard. He taught him how to skate, how to shoot, and how to pass. He often set up a table in

Wayne always loved to play hockey.

front of the goal net, so Wayne could shoot around it. That way, Wayne could practice by himself.

Walter would throw a puck into the corner of the rink and tell Wayne to get it. After Wayne chased several pucks around the boards, his father would say, "Watch me." He would throw the puck into the corner again and then skate to a spot where he would meet the puck as it flew around the boards. "I always told him, 'Skate to where the puck is going to be, not to where it has been,' " said Walter.

Wayne and his dad would go to hockey games together. As they drove home, Walter would ask Wayne if he remembered a certain play. Then they would talk about what each player did, or could have done. "I wanted Wayne to be aware of where every player was, all the time. His mind had to be like a camera. That would make his reaction time much quicker."

Wayne's reaction time was getting quicker, and soon he wanted to play in a youth hockey league. He was five years old. The rules said players had to be six. Wayne waited. The next year, he played. He scored only one goal that season. But he played so well that he made the Brantford Novice All-Star team. All the other boys on that team were ten or eleven years old!

In order to keep up with the older boys, Wayne practiced all the time. He would play with his friends after school. They played for two hours every afternoon, when there was ice. After dinner, Wayne went to his backyard to practice some more.

When Wayne wasn't playing hockey, he played other

sports. He was an excellent sprinter. Running helped build up his legs for skating. He also played lacrosse, another stick game. And he played baseball. He was such a good baseball player when he was older, that the Toronto Blue Jays wanted to sign him! But Wayne's first love was hockey.

A STAR IS BORN

When Wayne was seven, he scored 27 goals in the youth league. He was known as the kid who always had the puck. He was playing better than boys almost twice his age. The next year, as a small eight-year-old, Wayne scored 104 goals. As if that weren't enough, he scored 378 goals in 68 games the next season! Newspapers all over Canada were writing stories about him. Television reporters were following him, too.

Wayne loved the attention. He learned how to accept praise and sign autographs. There were problems, however. Wayne was always the youngest and smallest player on his team. Yet he scored the most goals. He was a rising star. The parents of some of the other players were jealous. "It's only human nature that people would resent him for scoring 200 or 300 goals in a season," said his father. "If your boy is on the team, you're not going to be happy."

Walter was thrilled with his son. Still, he understood why others were jealous. He told Wayne there would be many people who would give him special attention because he was so good. He also told his son that part of being a star was learning how to handle criticism. Wayne learned this lesson well. He was never a problem for his parents or his coaches.

Wayne was always under pressure. Everytime he played, people expected miracles. In spite of the pressure, Wayne wanted more competition. The Brantford league was too easy. So Wayne moved in with family friends in Toronto and played in a Junior B hockey league. He was only fourteen and away from home for the first time. Most of the other Junior B players were fifteen, sixteen, or seventeen. Wayne didn't have an easy time his first year in Toronto.

In his second year, things changed.

Wayne was small for his age. So one of his coaches told him to find a place on the ice where he wouldn't always get knocked down. Wayne went behind the net and stayed there. That was something new. Other offensive players had not considered staying behind the net.

A puck fired around the boards almost always passes behind the goal. So when Wayne was back there, he was easy to hit with a pass. The defenseman then had a problem. If he chased Wayne from one side of the net, Wayne would scoot out the other side. If two players came after him, one from either side, Wayne would slide the puck out to one of the empty areas. And if the other team left him alone behind the net, Wayne had time to thread a pass to someone's stick in front or come out in front of the net

Wayne learned the value of playing behind the net while playing Junior B hockey.

himself. Playing behind the net was like having an extra person on the ice.

Wayne's "new" position made him an even better player. He scored 70 goals and had 112 assists in his second year of Junior B hockey. He was a star again!

THE GREAT GRETZKY

Junior A hockey is the highest level for an amateur player under the age of twenty in Canada. When he was just sixteen, Wayne was chosen to play for the Junior A

Sault Sainte Marie Greyhounds. He moved to Sault Sainte Marie and again lived with family friends.

Wayne was the star of the Greyhounds. In the 1977-78 season, he set a new Ontario Hockey Association record of 182 points. He continued to charm the public and press. Fans loved him, especially boys his age. They saw him as a little guy outplaying big men.

Young boys and big men alike started calling Wayne "The Great Gretzky." The nickname came from a famous book, *The Great Gatsby*, by F. Scott Fitzgerald. Sportswriters started using the name, too. Before long, everyone used it.

The nickname wasn't the only thing Wayne was given in Sault Sainte Marie. He was given the uniform number 99. Some of the greatest hockey players in the history of the game had worn number 9—Gordie Howe, Maurice Richard, and Bobby Hull. Now Wayne was wearing two 9's, not just one. People thought he would someday be greater than the best players in hockey history.

At the age of sixteen, Wayne was famous, talented, and good looking. He could have dated just about any girl in Ontario. But he rarely even went on a date. He didn't drink, drive, or smoke. "My father always told me to get what I wanted most and the rest—girls, cars, money, and fame—would follow." Wayne said.

What Gretzky really wanted most was to sign with the pros. Finishing his high school education was not first on his list. Wayne did go to school though, while he played for the Greyhounds. By the end of his first season, he

After signing his pro contract, Wayne had breakfast with Nelson Skalbania, owner of the Racers.

needed only five more classes to graduate. However, he would turn pro before finishing the twelfth grade.

In 1978, there were two major hockey leagues. One was the National Hockey League (NHL), which began in 1917. The other was the World Hockey Association (WHA), which started in 1971. The Indianapolis Racers belonged to the WHA. They wanted to sign Wayne to their team. That presented a problem. Wayne was only seventeen, and the pros had agreed not to sign players that young. The Gretzkys and Wayne's agent, Gus Badali, fought that rule. They won! Wayne turned pro at the age of seventeen, signing a four-year contract worth $875,000.

PLAYING IN THE PROS

Everyone thought signing a 161-pound, seventeen-year-old to play in the pros was crazy. Wayne proved them wrong. He scored 3 goals and had 3 assists in 8 games for the Racers. Then the Racers' owner, Nelson Skalbania, sold Gretzky's contract to the Edmonton Oilers, because he needed money. The owner of the Oilers, Peter Pocklington, gave Gretzky a new contract. The contract was worth around $300,000 a year for twenty-one years. "Wayne Gretzky is the greatest young player in the world right now," said Pocklington. "One day, he'll likely be the oldest player!"

The Oilers took a big risk in signing Gretzky for such a long time. But a game against the Cincinnati Stingers in Gretzky's first season with the Oilers convinced the Oilers' coach, Glen Sather, that Gretzky was worth the risk. Gretzky wasn't playing good defense in the early part of that game. His poor playing cost the Oilers a goal. Sather benched Gretzky for more than a period. With the Oilers trailing 2-1, Sather sent Gretzky back in the game. He scored a "hat trick," (three goals), and the Oilers won 5-2! "He could have pouted and sulked," said Sather. "But when I put him back in, he scored a hat trick. That, to me, was the turning point of his pro career." Not just anyone could have been taken out of a game and then come back to score so many goals. But Wayne Gretzky wasn't just anyone.

Gretzky finished his first pro season with 110 points. He

*Wayne quickly showed the Oilers' owners that
he could play pro hockey.*

was named WHA Rookie of the Year. Just as important,
he didn't miss a game. He had proved he could handle the
faster pace and bigger players of the pro game. Anybody
who gets 50 goals in hockey is considered a superstar.
Gretzky scored 46 in only 80 games!

After the 1978-79 season, the WHA merged with the
NHL. The Oilers, with Gretzky, became one of the NHL's
new teams. Before the 1979-80 season began, few people
believed Gretzky could equal his scoring totals in the
NHL. The NHL players had little respect for the WHA.
They weren't about to give some eighteen-year-old kid

from the WHA the benefit of the doubt. They said Gretzky was "scrawny" and that he'd never tear up the league the way he did in the WHA. That was all Gretzky needed to hear.

GRETZKY AND THE NHL

Gretzky set a goal for himself. He wanted to get at least as many points in his first year in the NHL as he had in his WHA season. If he didn't, the NHL, the media, and the public would probably say he just wasn't good enough for the NHL. There was a lot of pressure on Gretzky. But he knew he could handle it. "I've had pressure all along," he said. "There's always going to be pressure on a professional athlete. I can't think about it."

Gretzky was right. He didn't have to think about the pressure. Despite a slow start in the NHL, Gretzky came on strong. He scored two goals and an assist in early November to help the Oilers defeat the powerful New York Islanders, 7-5. One night in February 1980, he tied a thirty-three-year-old record by getting seven assists in a single game. In that same game against the Washington Capitals, he set a single-season record for a rookie by getting his 96th point. A few days later, he became the youngest player ever to get 100 points in a season. (A point is given for each goal and each assist.) On April 2, he became the youngest player to score 50 goals in a season!

Wayne got seven assists in a single 1980 game.

Wayne was the youngest player to score 50 goals in a season.

Gretzky never doubted that he could achieve his goal of scoring at least as much as he did in the WHA. But even he was surprised at the kind of year he had. He tied for the league scoring championship with 137 points. Only Bobby Orr and Phil Esposito had ever scored more points. Gretzky was named the Most Valuable Player (MVP) in the league. He was awarded the Lady Byng Memorial Trophy, as the NHL's most gentlemanly player. The owner of the Oilers rewarded Gretzky with a Ferrari automobile.

THE 1980-81 SEASON

Still, some hockey people thought Gretzky's records were just luck. Before the 1980-81 season, few of the other teams' coaches accepted his abilities. They would defend against him as though he were just another player. They didn't believe he was the best offensive player in the game.

Gretzky started the 1980-81 season with a bang. He scored 12 points in the first four games. He scored in the next six games, too. By midseason, he had taken the NHL scoring lead from Marcel Dionne of Los Angeles.

Gretzky skated into NHL history by scoring five goals in a 7-5 victory over the Philadelphia Flyers. Four of the goals came within 7 minutes 58 seconds of play, making them the four fastest goals scored by a player. The four goals also tied the record for most goals in one period.

Gretzky kept right on going. About a month later, his 90th assist broke Bobby Clarke's record for most assists in

Wayne set a NHL record for assists during the 1980-81 season.

a season by a center. Gretzky would push that record to 109 before the season was over. He also set a record for most assists by any player, breaking the record of 102 set by Bobby Orr. Then he broke Phil Esposito's record for most points in a season, with 164!

THE 1981 STANLEY CUP PLAY-OFFS

It was Gretzky's performance in the play-offs that convinced everyone he was more than just a scorer. The Oilers finished the regular season in 14th place, with a 29-35-16 record. They played the Montreal Canadiens in the first round of the play-offs. Montreal had finished third, with a 24-1-2 record in its last 27 home games. The Canadiens had won four of the previous five Stanley Cups. Montreal was healthy, and they looked forward to an easy series against the Oilers. Montreal's goalie, Richard Sevigny, went so far as to say that Guy Lafleur, the Canadiens' leader, would put Gretzky "in his back pocket." That remark was a big mistake.

The Oilers beat Montreal 6-3 in the first game of the play-offs. Gretzky tied a Stanley Cup record by getting five assists. After the Oilers' sixth goal, Gretzky skated by the Canadien net and patted Sevigny in the area where his back pocket would be. Gretzky had made his point!

"Do you think anyone in the NHL believes this?" Gretzky asked after the Oilers beat Montreal 3-1 in the second game. Gretzky didn't believe it himself. Neither did the Canadiens. "All we've been doing is panicking when Gretzky's on the ice," said the Canadiens' center Keith Acton.

The Canadiens continued to panic in Game 3. Gretzky scored three of the Oilers' six goals to complete the sweep. The Oilers had a good time. When Gretzky was on the ice and the teams were at even strength, the Oilers outscored Montreal 11-0. Gretzky was super!

The Oilers played the New York Islanders, winners of the Stanley Cup the year before, in the next round of the play-offs. The Islanders' plan was to check (hit) Gretzky every chance they got. By the fifth and sixth games, Gretzky wasn't the same player he was in the first three or four. "They bumped him a lot more in the last few games," said coach Sather. "He was tired. He won't ever admit that to you. But then again, you can't rest him if he's the only guy winning games for you."

The Islanders won the series, 4-2. However, the series was a lot closer than New York had dreamed it would be. The Oilers and Gretzky had played well. They had shown the world that they were a team to watch.

A SEASON TO REMEMBER

Great hockey players hope to score 50 goals in a season. The best aim for 50 goals in 50 games. Up until the 1981-82 season, only two players got 50 in 50. Maurice Richard scored his 50 in 50 during the 1944-45 season. Mike Bossy reached his place in hockey history during the 1980-81 season. Wayne Gretzky skated into NHL history on December 31, 1981. He scored five goals in a 7-5 win over the Philadelphia Flyers. Those five goals gave him 50 goals in just 39 games!

Wayne had told the press that he would get 50 goals in his 47th game. His parents planned to watch him play that game in Toronto. His parents were as surprised as anyone. "I just couldn't believe it, when we heard he set the record against Philadelphia," Gretzky's father said. "It's hard to realize. But then Wayne called us from the dressing room. He sounded very tired."

After the game, Gretzky took the record in stride. "All I

Wayne shoots his record-breaking 77th goal past goalie Don Edwards.

want to do is help the team win," he said. But he did admit that scoring 50 goals in 39 games was probably the second biggest thrill of his NHL career. "It's the second best feeling I've ever had," he said. "It's not quite as thrilling as beating Montreal in the play-offs last year."

Before the 1981-82 season, Gretzky had said Phil Esposito's 76 goals in 78 games in 1970-71 was one record that might stand forever. Now he stood a good chance of breaking that record, too.

As Gretzky got closer to Esposito's record, Esposito began to follow him across Canada and the United States.

Phil wanted to be there if Wayne beat his record. "I am going to try to get the record quickly," said Gretzky. "I'd like to get it over with. I want these records out of the way as we head into the stretch."

ANOTHER RECORD

The first seven times that Gretzky shot the puck in the now famous game against Buffalo, the Sabres' goalie blocked it. Then, with less than seven minutes left in the game, Gretzky did what everyone had waited for him to do. He scored his 77th goal of the season, breaking Esposito's record.

Phil Esposito congratulates Wayne after he scored the 77th goal.

The record goal came at 13:24 of the last period. It was his eighth shot of the game. His ninth and tenth shots also got past the Sabres' goalie. Those goals gave him a total of 79 goals in 64 games.

President Reagan and his wife, Nancy, sent a telegram of congratulations. But the praise Gretzky seemed to appreciate most came from Don Edwards, the Sabres' goalie. Edwards skated the length of the ice to shake Gretzky's hand at the end of the game. Until that night, Edwards had held Gretzky to only 1 goal in 9 games over three seasons.

"The first thing that came into my head," said Gretzky after he scored the record-breaking goal, "was that it put us up, 4-3. Then there was relief and a sense of satisfaction. It took a lot of pressure off me."

Gretzky and Esposito sat together for interviews after the game. Gretzky wiped the sweat off of Esposito's forehead with a towel. "I happen to like him," Esposito said. Then he told a story. When Esposito was a star for the Boston Bruins, his father told him he had seen a fourteen-year-old named Gretzky playing for the Sault Ste. Marie Greyhounds. Esposito's father said that this kid named Gretzky "will break all your records someday." Just seven years later, it had happened!

Gretzky ended the 1981-82 season with 92 goals and 120 assists, for 212 points in 80 games. The NHL's second-leading scorer, Mike Bossy, had 65 points less. Gretzky now held twenty-seven NHL records. Gordie Howe was next with fourteen records. Gretzky had now been in the

Wayne celebrates after breaking another record!

league three years, and three times he was named its Most Valuable Player.

The NHL's Most Valuable Player ten years before, Bobby Orr, talked about Gretzky and his feats. "To me, what makes Wayne different is the little things," said Orr. "He's not real fast, but he's faster than you think. He doesn't have Bobby Hull's shot, but he shoots better than you think. He passes better than anybody I've ever seen. And he thinks so far ahead. People keep waiting for him to fall on his face. As long as he doesn't tire mentally, he'll play the game."

Many people said Gretzky was tired at the end of the year. The Oilers, who had finished second in the NHL, played 17th-place Los Angeles in the first round of the play-offs. The Oilers were upset in five games. Gretzky had five goals and seven assists in the series. He averaged 2.4 points per game, only slightly below his season average of 2.65. Gretzky had played well. The Oilers lost one game, 10-8, and another, 6-5, after leading 5-0. The defense just fell apart.

1982-83: GRETZKY KEEPS ON ROLLING

By December 1, 1982, Gretzky had made one or more goals or assists in every game of the season. In the game that night against the Philadelphia Flyers, he got two assists. He had scored in 27 straight games, one game less than the record of 28, held by Montreal's Guy Lafleur. Two games later, he broke Lafleur's mark. The streak finally ended at 30 against Los Angeles on December 9.

As of the middle of December, Gretzky was averaging 2.51 points a game. He was tied for second in the NHL with 26 goals. By the All-Star break, he had 137 points. He was far ahead of his nearest competitor. There was no doubt that he would win his third straight scoring title. The only question was by how much.

It would take a big effort to beat his totals of the

previous season, though. As of the All-Star break, Gretzky was 11 points back in total points. "It's not out of the question that I could break 212 points," said Gretzky, "but I'll need three points a game the rest of the way. I know if I only get 165 or 180 points, people are going to wonder what's wrong."

Nothing was wrong with Gretzky. He was still the best offensive player in the NHL. He was scoring a bit less because other teams and their coaches were finally taking him seriously. Other players were being paid good money to stop him. Often, Gretzky had two or three defensemen around him. It made his job harder, but not impossible.

As the regular season was coming to a close, the Oilers were in first place in their division. The team was assured of a place in the play-offs. Gretzky had scored 55 goals and had 101 assists. That left him 27 goals and 25 points behind his pace of the season before.

While Gretzky's goal total declined, two other Oilers, Jari Kurri and Glenn Anderson, scored their career highs. The Oilers, as a team, were averaging 5.29 goals a game. That was higher than the previous year's 5.21 average and not far from the NHL record of 5.38 goals, set by Montreal in 1919-1920. "I take what they give me," said Gretzky. "Any team that wants to send two men on me is going to leave somebody open. If I can get the puck to him, with the shooters on this team, it will probably be a goal. How I play the game depends on how the other team is playing me."

Other teams tried their best to keep the puck away from

During the 1982-83 season, teams started to put two or three defensemen around Wayne.

Wayne. They put their best players against him. Everyone tried to stop Gretzky. He couldn't be stopped!

No matter how other teams played him, Gretzky ended the season as the NHL scoring champion. He scored 71 goals and got 125 assists, for 196 points. He finished the season with five more assists than he'd had the year before.

THE 1983 PLAY-OFFS

The Oilers figured they had something to prove. They shocked the hockey world two years before when they knocked Montreal out of the play-offs in three games. Then they lost to the New York Islanders in the quarter-finals. And the next year, after winning their division, they lost in the first round of the play-offs to the Los Angeles Kings. The Oilers wanted to win the Stanley Cup this time around.

The Oilers played Winnipeg in the first round of the 1983 play-offs. Gretzky came out shooting. He scored four goals in the first game, as he led the Oilers to a 6-3 win. The Oilers kept on winning. They beat Winnipeg three straight games to win the series.

The Calgary Flames were next.

In the first two games against the Oilers, Calgary held Gretzky without a goal. But Calgary still lost both games. The Flames didn't want to think what would happen when Gretzky found the net. They found out in Game 3.

The Great Gretzky scored 4 goals and had 3 assists. He broke the play-off record for most points in a game and led the Oilers to a 10-2 win. Gretzky scored a hat trick at 4:53 of the second period. He scored his fourth goal on his fifth shot of the game with 54 seconds left in the second period. He broke the point record with just over a minute left to play in the game.

"We knew we had to play better than we did in previous series' to prove we were really a good hockey team," Gret-

Wayne in a face-off during the 1983 Stanley Cup finals.

zky said. "We went out after Winnipeg and won in three games. Now, we've won six in a row, and we don't want to stop."

There was no stopping the Oilers, at least not yet. Edmonton went on to win the series against Calgary, 4-1. Then they played the Chicago Black Hawks in the semifinals. Once again, it was the Oilers' series. Edmonton won four straight games. The Hawks didn't give up in any of the games. They just couldn't keep up with the Oilers. One sportswriter wrote that the Hawks "looked like square dancers compared to the Oilers' ballet."

The Oilers played the New York Islanders for the 1983 Stanley Cup. The Islanders had not played particularly well during the season. They had finished sixth in the

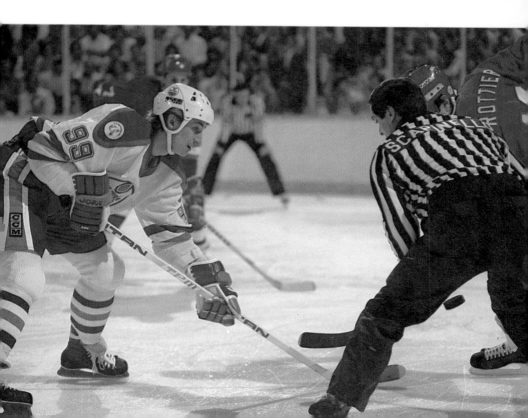

league. But they beat Washington, New York, and Boston to get to the finals of the Stanley Cup. The Islanders were the champions to beat, however.

What was billed as a "dream series" turned into a joke. The Islanders beat the Oilers in four straight games. The Oilers scored only six goals in four games. Gretzky was shut down completely. "My job is to put the puck in the net," said Gretzky after the series. "I just didn't." A shaken Wayne Gretzky ended the season, hoping that next year would be different.

Wayne shows the frustration of losing.

ENROUTE TO THE STANLEY CUP

Some hockey fans thought that Gretzky's poor performance in the 1983 Stanley Cup finals would hamper his play during the next season. How wrong they were! Nearly halfway through the 1983-84 season, Gretzky had scored at least one point in all 39 games. That was nine games beyond the old record he had set the season before. With 42 goals and 71 assists, Gretzky was ahead of his best pace. How long would the scoring streak last?

After scoring in 46 games, Gretzky admitted that the streak was putting a lot of pressure on him. "Every time I get that first point," he said, "I'm happy to get it over with. I hope there aren't too many like Chicago." He had scored in a Chicago game with only two seconds left to play!

Gretzky wasn't quite twenty-three years old, and only twenty-six players had scored more points in their entire careers than he had. Previously, the fastest player to score 900 points was Guy Lafleur. He did it in nine seasons. Gretzky would get 900 points before the end of his fifth season, more than four years ahead of Lafleur.

In the 1983-84 season, Gretzky recorded two eight-point games, one seven-point game and seven three-point games. He was chosen NHL player of the month for all three months of the season. Asked if his teammates were trying to help him out with more passes, Gretzky said, "Probably, but it's not glaring. We have a rule on this hockey team that we play as a team and not for individual records. We're just twenty guys doing a job, and the team has been playing so well that I feel I'm just one of the twenty."

If Gretzky felt he was just one of the twenty Oilers, he was the only one who thought so. Players, coaches, and other hockey observers were all talking about him. "He's unbelievable,'' said Steve Shutt of Montreal. "He's going to win two scoring titles this year—the NHL's and the NBA's (National Basketball Association)!'' Gretzky had now scored in 51 games in a row. That included 61 goals and 92 assists. If he continued that pace, he would beat the records he set in 1981-82.

Gretzky's streak ended at 51 games. He went scoreless in a game against the Los Angeles Kings on January 28, 1984. Still, he had beaten his own record of 30, set the year before. He had made the record book out-of-date!

Gretzky ended the season with 87 goals and 118 assists for a total of 205 points. He fell seven points short of his

amazing 1981-82 record. But that didn't seem to matter. The Oilers had finished in first place in their league and were anxious to try again to win the Stanley Cup.

Gretzky knew that all the records didn't mean as much as winning a Stanley Cup. He had said it himself. People weren't going to think as highly of him, until he brought the Cup to Edmonton.

THE STANLEY CUP BELONGS TO EDMONTON

The Oilers beat the Winnipeg Jets three games straight in the first round of the Stanley Cup play-offs. They then went on to win round two against the Calgary Flames, 4-3. Next they played the Minnesota North Stars in the semi-finals of the play-offs. The Oilers won the first two games. But Game 3 proved to be a difficult one. Edmonton went ahead 2-0 after one period. Then Minnesota exploded with five straight goals. But the Oilers showed their stuff by scoring six goals in a row, including five in the first eleven minutes of the third period. The Oilers won, 8-5.

"We just kept coming and coming," said Gretzky after the game. He had helped the Oilers win with a penalty shot goal in the third period. Gretzky called the Edmonton comeback "maybe the biggest we've ever had as a team."

Minnesota tried to become the third team in NHL history to rally from three games down in Game 4. Neither

Wayne scored in fifty-one straight games during the 1983-84 season to set another NHL record.

team scored for the first twenty-five minutes of the game. But five minutes into the second period, Oilers defenseman Don Jackson flicked in the first goal. Just seconds later, Ken Linseman of the Oilers made it 2-0. Each team scored one point in the third period to make the final score, Oilers 3, North Stars 1. The Oilers had swept the series and would meet the New York Islanders once again for the Stanley Cup.

The Oilers won the first game of the Stanley Cup finals, 1-0. At least one thing was for certain—the Oilers were not going to get swept four straight this time! The Oilers' win came on center Kevin McClelland's goal in the third period. The victory was the first against the Islanders in two-and-a-half years!

The Oilers celebrate after winning Game 1.

However, the Islanders evened the score by winning Game 2, 6-1. For the second straight game, Gretzky was held without a point. The New York crowds of 15,861 teased Gretzky, by chanting, "M-I-C-K-E-Y M-O-U-S-E!" They called him that because, earlier in the season, he had said that the New Jersey Devils were a "Mickey Mouse organization." The New York fans were getting back at Gretzky.

"I don't have any excuses," said Gretzky after Game 2. "I thought I was horrible, and I thought eighteen other guys on the ice weren't that good, either." All the Oilers knew they were going to have to play as a team, if they wanted to win. "If we think Gretzky is going to get the puck and go from our end in an end-to-end rush and

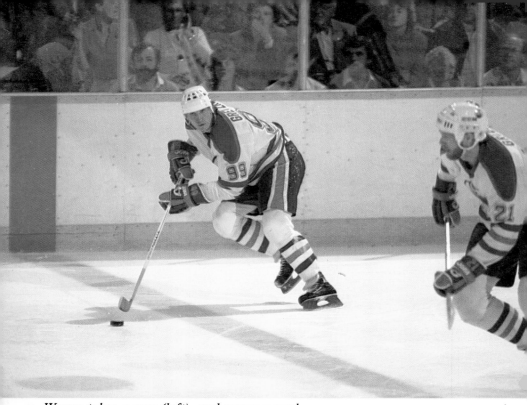

Wayne takes a pass (left), and scores a goal (right).

score, we are nuts,'' said Oilers' center Mark Messier. It was going to have to be a total team effort, or the Oilers would finish the season without the Stanley Cup.

The Oilers played good team hockey in Game 3. They blasted the Islanders 7-2. Gretzky helped set up what turned out to be the game winning goal in the second period. The Islanders were happy to finally get some goals. They looked forward to Game 4.

Gretzky broke out of his play-off slump and scored two goals in Game 4. The Oilers won, 7-2, and took a 3-1 lead in the Championship series. Gretzky's first goal came on a

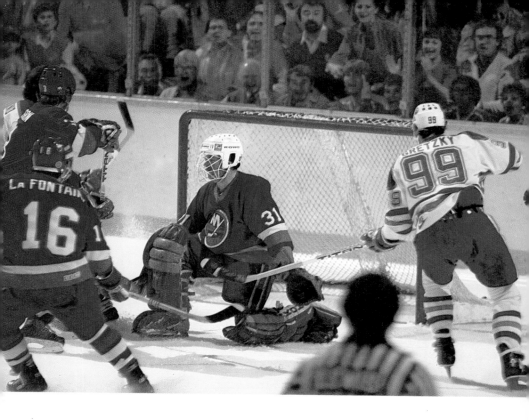

"breakaway" just 1:53 into the game. Gretzky was relieved to finally score. "That first goal was a great relief. I knew my teammates were wondering when Gretzky was going to score."

Islander captain Denis Potvin blamed himself for the defeat. He and his defense partner, Ken Morrow, were caught "up ice" on Gretzky's first goal. "His goal set the tone," said Potvin, "and it was my fault. I wasn't where I was supposed to be."

To keep their hopes alive, the Islanders needed the most dramatic comeback in the finals since the Toronto Maple

Teammates congratulate Wayne after he scored a goal.

Leafs rallied after being down 0-3 forty two years before. The Oilers had backed them into a do-or-die corner. But the Islanders had experience behind them. They had won the Stanley Cup four times; the Oilers had never won. "It's going to be exciting for the Oilers from the drop of the puck," said the Islanders' player-coach Butch Goring. "I am sure they are going to want the Cup pretty badly. That means they will feel the pressure."

If the Oilers felt the pressure in Game 5, they didn't show it. New York's Paul Boutilier skated deep into the Oilers' zone, midway through the first period. Boutilier lost the puck behind the Oilers' net. Then he ran into Oiler goalie Andy Moog and was going to be penalized. But before the Islanders could touch the puck to stop play, Jari Kurri fed Gretzky for a breakaway. "The Great Gretzky" put in a wrist shot for the first goal of the game.

Just over five minutes later, the Oilers raced down the ice. Kurri fed Gretzky, who flipped a twenty-foot shot past goalie Smith. That put the Oilers up, 2-0. By early in the second period, the Oilers were ahead, 4-0.

The Islanders came back and scored two goals in the opening thirty-five seconds of the third period. But the Oilers settled down after that. They held the Islanders for the rest of the game. With just 13 seconds left, Oiler Dave Lumley found an empty net and scored. The Oilers had won Game 5, 5-2, and the Stanley Cup!

In front of a screaming Edmonton crowd of 17,498, Gretzky was presented the Cup by league president, John Ziegler. "You spend years and years of work and you

44

The Oilers hold up the Cup for their fans!

finally win the Stanley Cup,'' said Gretzky. "There is nothing else like it.'' While the Islanders wept in the dressing room, the Oilers and their fans celebrated their long-awaited victory.

THE GENIUS

Athletes such as Wayne Gretzky don't come along very often. Such athletes are the best in their sport. Take Babe Ruth, for example. In 1921, he had 60 home runs. The Number Two home run hitters, Bob Meusel and Ken Williams, had only 24.

Wilt Chamberlin averaged a record 50.4 points a game for Philadelphia during the 1961-62 National Basketball Association season. Walt Bellamy was next at 31.6 points a game.

O.J. Simpson of the Buffalo Bills set his National Football League rushing record of 2,003 yards in 1973. That was nearly double the total yards of John Brockington, who finished in second place with 1,144 yards!

What sets Wayne Gretzky apart is that, physically, he is nowhere as strong as the Babe, as large as Wilt Chamberlin, or as fast as O.J. Simpson. From the time he learned to skate, all he heard was that he was "too small and too skinny.'' But he has proved the doubters wrong.

"The Great Gretzky'' is on his way to becoming the best hockey player of all time!

The "Great Gretzky" is becoming the best hockey player of all time!

47

WAYNE GRETZKY'S PROFESSIONAL STATISTICS

WHA

Year	Team	Goals	Assists	Total Points
1978-79	Indianapolis	3	3	6
1979-80	Edmonton	43	61	104

NHL

Year	Team	Goals	Assists	Total Points
1980-81	Edmonton	55	109	164
1981-82	Edmonton	92	120	212
1982-83	Edmonton	71	125	196
1983-84	Edmonton	87	118	205